RANDOM REFLECTIONS

Jameel Ahmed Khan

INDIA • SINGAPORE • MALAYSIA

ISBN
Paperback 979-8-89588-368-6
Hardcase 979-8-89610-714-9

Poetry collection complete.

The Random Reflections poetry book.

CONTENTS

SECTION 1-14 RANDOM CONNECTIONS

Section 15-23 Relationship

Section 24-47 Self-Reflections

Section 48-52 Romance

Section 53-56 Reflections of Society

SECTION 57-60 SOME MORE

SECTION 61-64 FANTASY

Section 1-14
Random Connections

1.

DOTS

He, who was deeply saddened by his failure,
Felt something inside.
When he looked back,
The dots formed
As he connected them,
And he realised.

2.

AWARENESS

Luxury seems like autocratic power,
Its impact is felt by the majority.
Luxury appears significant, but it is not.
Owning luxury seems motivating to some,
But it has harmed –
Harmed the power
To recognise limitless boundaries,
Boundaries restricted by luxury.
He felt all this within the brand.
And moved on, smiling and smoking.
A sad, depressed intellect he is.
But it's good to know he is aware.

3.

SMOKE AND YOU

Days have passed since I last smoked.
After hearing a woman cry,
A cry that pierced my soul,
A soul that is pure, soft but directionless.
A woman I lost, but in losing, I won.
A win that is sad, depressing, yet life-saving.
He thought and he smiled.

4.

HEARTS

In the quiet of a breaking dawn,
Two hearts sat, worlds apart, yet near,
Words once whispered are now heavy stones,
The echoes of a love turned sheer.
Silence, thick like a morning mist,
Wrapped around their aching pride,
Their wounded souls, their clenched fists –
All the pain they tried to hide.
But as shadows danced in the flickering light,
They saw the truth in soft, trembling eyes,
The hurt that came from holding tight,
To anger, to ego, to desperate lies.
And so, they listened—not to reply,

But to understand the other's pain,
Letting old grievances drift by.
Like leaves falling in autumn rain.
They found each other in the quiet space,
Where love could mend what fear had torn,
Two hearts saved by a listening grace,
By letting go, they were reborn.

5. DEEP WITHIN ME

I smell the dark but refuse to become it,
I consume enough, yet never feel full,
I chase after you, but you don't see,
I am your inner self, led by ego's pull.
Ego, a charming thief, so sly,
Destroying life, devouring thought,
Yes, you and I are one and the same,
Yet so different, each battle fought.
I love to silence the voice of innocence,
To cloud your mind, to blur the light,
And you, the innocent one, I seek to change,
Still stand against me, still hold tight.

6.

IN THE JUNGLE OF THOUGHTS

In the midst of a jungle, you and I,
Thinking of faults in thee –
A mirror shows what could have been.
No separation, no war, just happiness.
Why would I write this?
If not for going through this?

7.

REFLECTING ON THE PAST

Thinking of the past might tense you,
But it also makes you realise your faults.
Two sides of a coin – one bad, one good.
Put yourself in others' shoes,
And see how much time they have for you.

8.

THE LIGHT OUTSIDE

It's been dark all day,
Until I realised the light is outside.
To get sunlight, I must step out.
To be bright, I must take pride.

9.

RAINY SEASON MELODIES

Water droplets fall, splashing,

Sounds on stone, leaves and roofs,

Crickets and frogs join the symphony,

Yes, it's the rainy season.

Paper boats sail through without a mission.

10.

DEBATES AND FOOLS

A topic starts, a debate darkens.
Raised voices, red faces –
Reason diluted, a brawl finishes all.

11.

STAY

On the verge of jumping,
Cutting hands, ending life—
A troubled mind, just sleep, and say no to dying.

12.

A CHILD'S STORY

He, who was a child, bullied and feared,
Felt deprived, always on edge –
Now, waiting for those smiles.
That makes him forget his crime.

13.

WOUNDS AND SORROW

Wounds won't heal by showing,
Sorrow won't be erased but by erasing.
What will crying and grief give?
Snatch your rights from the world.

14.

DESIGNING DREAMS

Let's design a dream once more,
Keep up with life,
The town will build itself.
Let's dwell in the desert;
People will come along.
Let's build the caravan.
By Majid Khalil

Section 15-23
Relationship

15.

BEGINNING

You and I seemed perfect, a flawless match,
A rose in hand, kneeling before you,
Waiting for those words to come forth –
And yes, the journey began.

16.

CONVERSATIONS AND LONGINGS

Days remain, time slips through our hands.
To be close to thee, long talks aren't enough.
Feels like all I need is to meet, to see –
Oh, you perfect lady,
Your words, a soothing song,
You care for me as if you are me, not thee.

17. THE MEETING

The day arrives:
The meeting of the bee and the flower,
With a smile on your face, you said, "Yes."
Happiness surrounds,
Birds sing, music fills our ears.
Though not real, still, we see it clearly –
Family and friends celebrate,
As the sun sets and the moon rises,
Just you and me, in a room alone.
Smiling, hiding behind our faces,
We draw closer and spend the night.

18.

PARTINGS AND PROMISES

Heart says stay,

Mind says go –

To leave, even for a moment, feels impossible.

But to work is to eat.

Oh, honey, take care,

I'll be back soon,

In no time, right here.

19.

UNCONDITIONAL LOVE

Dinner is served –
Oops, no salt, but it's okay.
We sprinkle a little,
Oh, you girl,
You've made my life heavenly.
We are together in a unconditional contract.

20.

LOVE AT FIRST SIGHT

Days pass,
A bee and a flower meet in the garden.
When the bee came,
It was for nectar and love at first sight.
Blind to faults,
Everything was clear; nothing was hidden.

21.

ACCEPTANCE AND UNDERSTANDING

Wearing each other's shoes,
Turning the tables, removing the trouble,
Accepting faults in you and me –
It makes sense; it saved us.
We laughed; there's no need for judgement.
It's life; we all experience it.

22.

CONFLICTS AND EGOS

You pointed at me, and I pointed at you.
Chaos ensued.
How can I be less than thee?
Come, let's race; it feels unjust.
Those points were love in disguise.
Now, they are cases of irritation.
A five-letter word, a saviour of relations –
Why are we so far from it?
Bowing before the one we love –
Why wage war against them?

23.

THE REALISATION

You earned my love;
I found you through the trials.
It was fresh. Life felt small,
No faults, no troubles –
Just the joy of meeting,
Bee and flower, again and again.

SECTION 24-47
SELF-REFLECTIONS

24.

SMOKE

The Smoke of Regret

A pot full of smoke shows the trail,
Fading lungs, coughing voice,
Plans fail for the fun that turns to pain,
Ticking clock, time to bid goodbye.

UNKNOWN

Searching for the Unknown
Not knowing the coast,
Still searching for a host –
Trying to put limits on the limitless.

26.

THE SILENCE OF YOURS

The silence of yours was my deep desire.

Running between the line, I read you behind the line.

Upon feeling your existence, I visualised the date with me. Nothing much has happened since then.

Except a journey within me.

27.

IN THE MIDST OF THE WAY

In the midst of the way,

Sleep takes over these eyes.

And dreams knocked on his door. Spending a whole life was worth.

But waking up to reality was a dream.

28.

THE SOUND OF SOLITUDE

The sound of solitude.
Asleep on a plane, he dreamed of a day,
A day he never planned to visit.
Not moving was an option, but he chose,
Dark nights became friends with him when asked.
Indeed, it was all planned like a spider's web.
The way he had was always right, but he never chose, though.

THE CHOSEN PATH

The chosen path is a journey to the treasure.

Waiting on the coast is a priceless emotion. "Does anything matter at all?" he asked.

"Yes, it's only you who is a fool," replied the wave.

"Okay, then I should spend it," he said.

It's with him all the way, he found.

30.

WAS IT A FAULT?

Was it a fault?

No, he replied.

Is it just a mistake?

What's the difference between the two?

Just a point of view, he sighed.

31.

THE WEIGHT OF WORDS

Words carry weight; they can build or destroy.
A sentence, a paragraph, a page –
All can form bridges or ignite fires.
He knew this, but often forgot –
Lost in translation, meaning came and went.

32.

THE TRUTH UNSEEN

We seek truth in a world of lies,
Blind to what's in front of our eyes.
Each step forward seems like a mile,
But the truth is hidden in a smile.

33.

LIFE'S BITTER LESSON

Life teaches in ways harsh and rough –
It shows the value of being soft with tough.
But in the bitterness, sweetness hides,
Lessons learned are where truth abides.

34.

QUESTIONS OF EXISTENCE

Why are we here? What's the point?
A search for meaning in every joint.
The answer lies in what we give,
Not in how we die, but in how we live.

35.

HOPE IN DESPAIR

In the darkest nights, hope appears,
A small glimmer amidst the tears.
He held it tight, refused to let go –
In the end, it's all he needed to grow.

36.

THE COURAGE WITHIN

Fear gripped him tightly, his heart raced fast.
But courage within stood up at last.
He faced the storm, the wind, and the rain –
And found himself through all the pain.

37.

THE VOID INSIDE

An empty space he felt within,
A void he tried to fill with sin.
But in the end, he learned this truth:
It's love and peace that feed our youth.

38.

LIFE'S GENTLE WHISPER

Life whispers softly, gently so,
Telling secrets only the quiet know.
He stopped and listened, heard it clearly –
The meaning of life is always near.

AGAINST THE TIDE

Swimming upstream, against the flow,
It's hard, it's painful, but you grow.
He chose his path, not the easy way –
And found himself in the struggle each day.

40.

A CHILD'S SMILE

A child's smile, pure and bright,
A beacon of hope in the darkest night.
He saw it once and never forgot,
The simplest joy, a priceless thought.

41.

TIME'S GENTLE HANDS

Time moves with hands so slow,
But leaves behind a heavy blow.
He felt its weight, learned its grace,
That time is precious, can't be replaced.

42.

DREAMS ON PAPER

He wrote his dreams on a white paper,
Hoping they'd take off, soar in flight.
But dreams, he learned, are like the wind –
They shift and change, never pinned.

43.

THE MIRROR'S TRUTH

He looked in the mirror and saw a face,
Lines of worry, years to trace.
But in the eyes, he found the spark,
A flame of hope, a light in the dark.

44.

THE JOURNEY'S END

The journey's end is never clear,
But it's not the end that we should fear.
It's missing the beauty along the way –
The laughs, the tears, the light of day.

45.

LOST AND FOUND

He lost himself in a sea of doubt,
But in the loss, he found the route.
To self, to love, to endless skies –
To the truth that lies within him.

46.

THE PATH OF FORGIVENESS

Forgiveness is a path not paved,
It's hard to walk, but it's how we're saved.
He chose it once, then twice again –
And found in it the end of pain.

47.

THE FINAL WHISPER

At the end of it all, when all is done,
The battle fought, the war won.
He heard a soft and true whisper –
"Life was beautiful because of you."

Section 48-52
Romance

48.

TO MY LOVE

To my love,
My Lucy, my divine,
A charming, unpredictable arrival,
You act like no one else.
Every thought of yours,
Keeps me gazing,
Lost in the way you react,
The way you listen,
The way your eyes speak –
I wonder if I do not have you
It would be my saddest story.
You've touched my soul.
In ways you don't even know.
Why do I see you like this?

You'd need my eyes to understand.
Thank you for arriving unexpectedly,
Thank God for making you this way –
A charm among millions,
A one-in-a-billion kind.
I'm sorry, I cannot explain.
Why I'm good enough?
For a soul like yours,
And why you need me
Like a pole,
Drawing in the future.
In silence,
Complete.

49.

THE DESIRE

Let's make a deal –
A deal to be together,
An hour of a full life,
An hour of half-cooked meals.
Let's make a deal to share a space,
Yet, allow each other space.
Not roaming, just an idea,
To sit still and relax.
Let's make a deal –
A deal to refine life,
And define death.
A death with your hand in mine,
Ending our story,
But with a happy ending.

Let's make a deal
To be more than soulmates,
To be mates who act like strangers,
Yet share the same mind,
Two parts of one whole.
Let's end this poetry.
In silence.

50.

THE GAME OF LIFE

Let us play the game of life –
Who are you, and what's your kind?
Let's play a game of checkmate.
While indulging in the wine,
The wine of patience,
A cool way to strive.
Are you the coolest girl I know?
Yes, indeed – yet not mine, too.
I hope that tomorrow, as the sun shines,
We will be gazing at it together,
But from afar.

51.

GIRL

Hey, girl,
I want to indulge in cheating –
Cheating myself,
Believing you are mine.
I want to hold onto wrongs and leave the rights,
I want to disrupt the market,
The market of love, by being a cheater –
A self-bragger who holds you in dreams.
But not in reality.
Hey, let's sleep apart tonight,
In our separate beds,
And meet each other in dreams.
Silence.

52.

YOU

In your presence, time slows and hearts race,
You entered, effortlessly captivating the space.
Your gaze, a symphony, listening with intent,
Each gesture, each word, is a testament.

Though I may not match your stride or grace,
I strive to impress, longing to embrace.
Dreaming of waking by your side each day,
Your smile is my compass, lighting the way.

Together, mornings would be a cherished delight,
Preparing breakfast, bathed in the morning light.
From morning tea to day's end, in sweet moments,
With you, my world is complete, our journey replete.

Section 53-56
Reflections of Society

53.

AN ALTER EGO SMASHED BY LIGHT

An alter ego was shattered by the light,
Awakening the demon –
A demon who speaks,
But is deaf.
His emotions flare, lighting up the theatre,
A place where goodness and intellect,
Are dissected and displayed.
Far from the stream, a beggar sits,
Watching the entertaining game.
Suddenly, the lights go out. The cinema is silenced.
Everyone wakes to the truth –
The source of their jealousy.
The crowd is hushed,
Left only with hope.

54.

THUNDERSTORM

The thunderstorm cracked like a drummer's beat,
In a small hall filled with people,
Engaged in chatter –
The talk of the crowd,
A game that ruled the nation.
Nearby played a boy, gentle and kind,
Much like the others had been.
Some years ago.
The trees encircling the compound,
We're withering away,
Dying from the curses of the people.
Everything in this scene seemed strangely normal,
Yet dark when one thought of its depths.
He smoked alone in the bedroom,

Far from the hall –
Then drifted off to sleep.
The game continues tomorrow.

55.

THE BET

Whoever ate the meat,
Met their death –
Or so, the rumour spread.
Through the valley.
A farmer heard it and wagered.
He would live, he would win.
Few were interested, save a rich boy –
The bet was set.
The day came,
And no one ever saw the farmer again.
The boy claimed, "Perhaps he died,"
But the farmer's death was different.
In life and death, he found his chance,
He tried to squeeze it tightly,

But failed, for he couldn't measure.
The worth of money or the weight of the bet.
The ink ran dry; the writer set down his pen,
Hoping to end the suspense someday.

56. THE WALL

Let's build the wall.
So we can fight fiercely to destroy it someday.
Let's make a deal,
So, we can think deeply and become wise.
Let's dry the leaf and wait for its death,
Then blame the tree.
And yes, let's just write this,
Knowing everything –
Yet, being too afraid to die.

Section 57-60
Some More

57.

LAMP

The lamp was talking to the wall.

This hadn't happened in a long while.

Silence grew curious, wanting to know itself.

The lamp guided the way and then switched off along the way.

58.

ME

Splashing the truth, my intellect.
Dove deep into my foolishness.

I read the facts, then tossed the chewing gum,
Into the void of space.

I stayed blind throughout.
Only keeping in touch with your face.

59.

NOSTALGIA

Through the pavements,

It flows down the road.

Kids playing around haven't forgotten their paper boats;

The rainy atmosphere is rich with laden desires.

Long had it gone with the winds,

Leaving the players alone on the pitch.

60.

TIME

The dark path cries out in pain,
A sudden death, but a sweet hidden move—
A move into the jungle of the past,
The past that fed your inner desires.
Upon opening the door, you are amazed,
Amazed by the beauty of the connected dots,
Dots linking the past to the future,
With the rain running behind,
A period that silently follows.

Section 61-64
Fantasy

61.

PATH

The dark path cries out in pain.
The sudden death, but a sweet hidden move.
A move to the jungle of the past.
The past that fed your inner desires.
Upon opening the door, you are amazed.
Amazed by the beauty of the connection of the dots.
The dots from the past to the future.
And the rain running behind.
Period that silently follows.

62.

LETTERS

Dear Oliver, take care,

The last message you recorded for her is destined to remain unseen.

The girl you wish to give space and smiles,

The girl you wish to care for and give hope,

Does not exist.

Thousands of girls try to escape toxic relationships and dominating partners.

One could have found you, so you both could smile, but that fate is non-existent.

Your longing to put a smile on her face Every day, from dawn to dusk,

Exists in a fate that is not real.

Providing her space and care, making her smile, is a dream that fades.

Do you know why?

Because the eyes to see your longing heart
do not exist.

Those who exist do not know you because
you are alone,

And your fate is non-existent.

63.

DREAM

"The breakfast I made for you was amazing," you said.

The bed tea wasn't perfect, but you smiled.

You loved the meals I crafted, the cookies I baked.

After all, I am a baker's son.

But when I woke, you were gone, leaving behind only a plate.

With leftover food in a hotel room.

64.

HOPE

People laugh at me when they see the ring
for the girl who doesn't exist. But having
this ring with me, I feel the touch of yours,

A non-existent love,

Putting me in the zone of hope-

A hope that allows me to live again.

www.ingramcontent.com/pod-product-compliance
Lightning Source LLC
La Vergne TN
LVHW091120150826
845673LV00002B/899

* 9 7 9 8 8 9 5 8 8 3 6 8 6 *